What Is the Sign for Friend?

by Judith E. Greenberg

photographs by Gayle Rothschild

Carin Bea Feldman, Consultant

Franklin Watts
New York/London/Toronto/Sydney/1985

Library of Congress Cataloging in Publication Data

Greenberg, Judith E.
   What is the sign for friend?

   Summary: Text and photographs depict the life of
Shane, a deaf child who goes to a regular school and
enjoys normal activities with the help of sign language
and a hearing aid.
   1. Children, Deaf—Juvenile literature. 2. Deaf—
Means of communication—Juvenile literature. [1.
Deaf. 2. Physically handicapped] I. Rothschild, Gayle,
ill. II. Title.
HV2392.G74   1985   362.4'2'088054   84-26986
ISBN 0-531-04939-6

For Roger and Shari—
because they listen

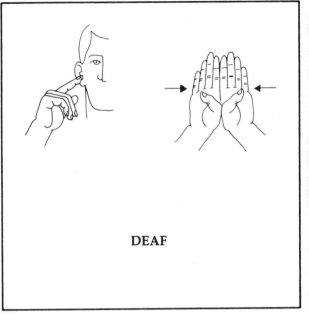

DEAF

Shane loves soccer, insects, pizza, and computer games. He was born deaf, but he can do almost everything that his hearing friends can.

Shane likes to go out with his parents and his sister, Mimi. For a special treat they sometimes stop at a pizza restaurant for lunch. Shane reads the menu and orders his favorite pizza—pepperoni and mushroom.

Mimi taps Shane gently when the waitress is ready to take his order because he doesn't hear her speak to him. He doesn't hear the music playing softly in the background, either.

PIZZA

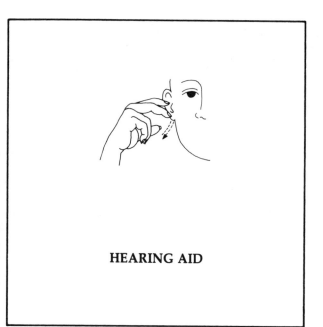

HEARING AID

When Shane was a baby, three months old, his mother discovered that he couldn't hear her singing him to sleep. At naptime, even the noise of the vacuum cleaner under his crib didn't wake him.

Shane's doctor arranged for him to see Mrs. Brecker. She is an audiologist. Her job is to help people who can't hear well. Mrs. Brecker tested Shane's hearing and found out that he could not hear any sounds or voices. Mrs. Brecker fitted Shane with a hearing aid that helps him hear better. Even with the hearing aid, no sound is completely clear. He wears his hearing aid every day.

SCHOOL

Shane has many friends. Some of his friends are deaf; some are not.

Several children in Shane's school are deaf. They have some classes together, but they spend most of the day in classes with children who can hear.

12

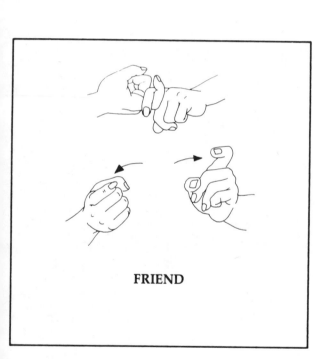

FRIEND

Mitchell is one of Shane's best friends. They met at a gymnastic club where they learn to jump on the trampoline and balance on a beam. When Shane can't hear the instructor's directions, Mitchell shows him what to do.

Shane and Mitchell like to ride their bicycles together. Mitchell listens carefully for cars when he rides in the street. Shane can't hear the cars, so a sign near his house tells drivers to look out for him.

15

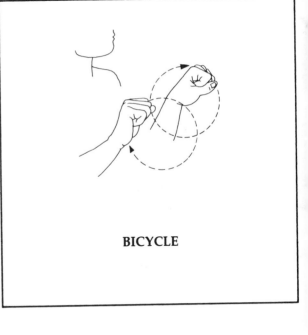

BICYCLE

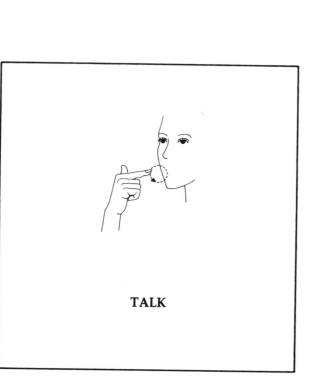

TALK

Shane can't hear other people's voices very well, so he has had trouble learning to talk himself. Sometimes his voice sounds very high and he doesn't always make all the sounds in a word. His voice sounds different from his friends' voices and they have a hard time understanding him.

Ms. Smith is a speech therapist who is helping
Shane improve his speech. She is teaching him
to know how loudly he is speaking and how to
form sounds. Shane is learning to see the sounds
of words on Ms. Smith's lips. When he says a
word correctly, Ms. Smith smiles and gives him a
sticker for his collection. He practices the word
with Ms. Smith and later he practices at home
with his mother.

17

WORD

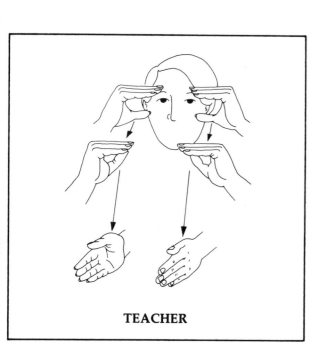

TEACHER

Ms. Hill is another person who helps Shane. She is an expert in sign language. At school, Ms. Hill stands next to Shane's teacher and interprets everything she says to the class. Shane sits in the front of the room where he can see his teacher and Ms. Hill very clearly. Ms. Hill uses her hands and facial expressions to repeat the lesson in sign language. Shane also watches her mouth because Ms. Hill silently repeats the teacher's words. Watching Ms. Hill's lips, her hand signs, and her facial expressions, Shane follows the lesson along with his classmates.

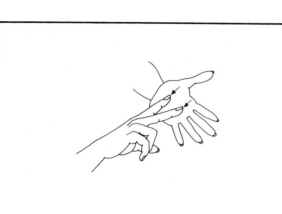

READ

Another way that Shane learns is by cued speech. Ms. Hill uses her hands and lips to show Shane the sounds that the letters make. This has helped him learn to read. Reading is Shane's favorite subject. He loves books about insects.

20

Some other subjects are hard for Shane. It's
difficult for him to write sentences by himself.
He doesn't always hear every word in a sentence
and sometimes he forgets to write all the
words—especially small words like *a*, *the*, and *of*.

21

WRITE

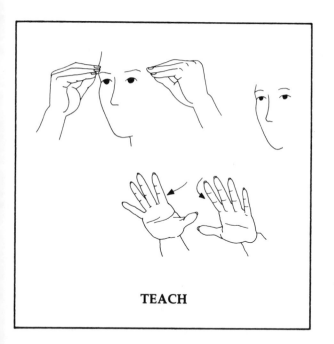

TEACH

After school Shane and Mitchell play on a neighborhood soccer team. Shane can hear the referee's whistle, but he can't hear his teammates if they call to him. With everyone cheering, he can't hear the coach telling him what to do. He has to watch the ball very carefully to know if someone is about to pass the ball to him. Shane's friends think he is a good player because he scored ten goals last season.

Mitchell is also a good soccer player, and the boys like to practice their kicking and passing together.

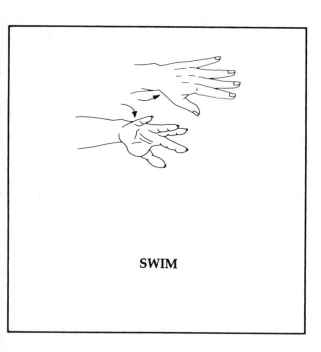

SWIM

Swimming is another favorite activity for Shane and Mitchell. They love to jump in the pool with a big splash. Mitchell hears the sound of the splash, but Shane can only see the water fly high in the air. Shane can't wear his hearing aid in the pool because it isn't waterproof.

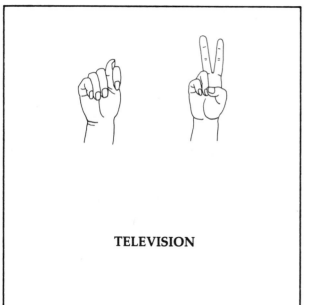

TELEVISION

When the boys watch television, Shane usually has someone interpret for him. His mother often helps him understand the show by signing the words he cannot hear. Sometimes Shane watches the picture and makes up his own stories.

Sometimes Shane uses a special device that helps him understand television shows. When a program is marked "closed captioned" he can use this device to read the words on his television screen.

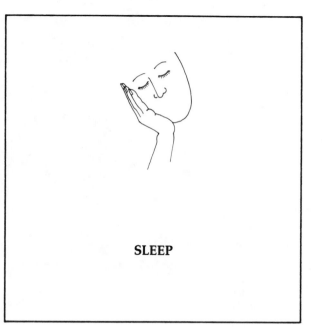

SLEEP

Mitchell likes to spend the night at Shane's house. When the boys go to bed, Shane takes his hearing aids out of his ears before he goes to sleep.

At night Shane's world is completely silent. He doesn't hear

his dad snoring, or

the clock ticking, or

the rain falling against his

windowpane, or

his mom tiptoeing in to cover him

up.

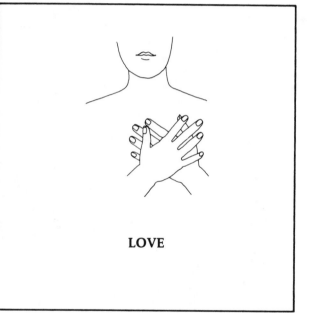

LOVE

In the morning, Shane doesn't need an alarm clock! His dog Abby wakes him up right on time.

Shane also has a funny striped cat named Scooba. He talks to his pets to practice speaking. Abby and Scooba don't care what Shane says to them. They only care that he loves them. No one needs words to feel love.

ABOUT THE AUTHOR

Judith E. Greenberg is a graduate of Trenton State College in New Jersey. A former social studies teacher, she has co-authored several books for Franklin Watts, including the recently published *Jewish Holidays* and *How to Participate in a Group, How to Read a Newspaper*, and *How to Use Primary Sources* in Watts' Social Studies Skills series. Ms. Greenberg lives in Potomac, Maryland.

ABOUT THE PHOTOGRAPHER

Gayle Rothschild is a graduate of Syracuse University and holds a Master of Fine Arts degree from the University of Maryland. Her photographs have appeared in a variety of publications, including *The Washington Post*. A former elementary school teacher, Ms. Rothschild lives in Potomac, Maryland, with her husband and two children.

ABOUT THE CONSULTANT

Carin Bea Feldman graduated from Adelphi University and holds an M.A. degree from Brooklyn College. She is an instructor at Montgomery College in Rockville, Maryland, and works with deaf children as a speech pathologist. Mrs. Feldman is married and the mother of two children.